The science in...

...a
BICYCLE

The science of forces and more...

Ian Graham

W
FRANKLIN WATTS
LONDON•SYDNEY

First published in 2008
by Franklin Watts

Copyright © Franklin Watts 2008

Franklin Watts
338 Euston Road
London NW1 3BH

Franklin Watts Australia
Level 17/207 Kent Street
Sydney, NSW 2000

Planning and production by
Discovery Books Limited
Editor: Rebecca Hunter
Designer: Keith Williams
Illustrator: Stefan Chabluk
Photo researcher: Rachel Tisdale

Dewey number 531'.118

ISBN 978 0 7496 8239 2

Printed in China

Franklin Watts is a division of Hachette
Children's Books, an Hachette Livre UK
company. www.hachettelivre.co.uk

Photo acknowledgements: Corbis/Jamie Kripke, front cover top & bottom right; istockphoto.com/Andrew Howe, front cover bottom left; Getty Images/Hulton Archive, p. 4; Getty Images/Paul Chesley, p. 5; istockphoto.com/VikaValter, p. 6; istockphoto.com/Michael Smith, p. 7; istockphoto.com/Oleg Kozlov, p. 8; Rebecca Hunter, p. 9; Getty Images/Ariel Skelley, p. 10; Getty Images/John Nordell/The Christian Science Monitor, p. 11; Discovery Picture Library, p. 12; istockphoto.com/Silvia Jansen, p.13 top; Getty Images/Doug Pensinger, p.13 bottom; istockphoto.com/Mario Savoia, p. 15; Getty Images/Barry Durrant, p. 16; istockphoto.com/Martin Krammer, p. 17 top; Rebecca Hunter, p. 17 bottom; istockphoto.com/Maxim Petrichuk, p. 19; Discovery Picture Library, p. 20; Discovery Picture Library, p. 21; istockphoto.com/Kledge, p. 22; istockphoto.com/James Ferrie, p. 23 top; istockphoto.com/Shariff Che'lah, p. 23 bottom; Rebecca Hunter, p. 24; CFW Images/Chris Fairclough, p. 25; istockphoto.com/Andrew Howe, p. 27 top; Getty Images/Javier Soriano, p. 28; Corbis/Olivier Labalette/TempSport, p. 29 top; Corbis/Duomo, p. 29 bottom

Contents

Words that appear in **bold** are in the glossary on page 30.

A bike

There's a lot of science in your bike. Keeping a bicycle upright, pedalling and turning corners without falling over is a careful balancing act – and you do it all without having to think about it!

Shape

Bikes have been around for a long time. The first two-wheelers were made in the early 1800s and bikes are still very popular today. In fact, more than 1 billion bikes exist in the world today, with another 100 million being made each year.

Bikes didn't always look like they do today. Designers have tried making bikes in different shapes. One of the strangest was the penny-farthing or high-wheeler. The rider sat perched on top of a huge front wheel up to 1.5 metres high, with a tiny wheel at the back. However, bike designers and riders soon found that the best bikes have a diamond-shaped frame, with the rider sitting between two wheels that are the same size.

◄ Penny-farthing bikes were fast, but getting on them was tricky. The rider had to climb up on top of the giant front wheel and start pedalling before the bike fell over!

▶ *In parts of China, India and other countries, there are few cars, so bicycles or tricycles are still the most common way to get around.*

Strength

If you look at a bike's diamond frame more closely, you'll see that it is made of two triangles back to back (below).

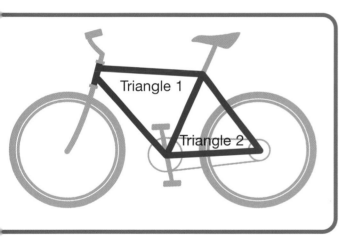

Triangle 1

Triangle 2

Triangles are very strong shapes. They can't be pushed out of shape without changing the length of one of their sides or breaking one of the joints between the sides. Look at steel bridges and towers and you'll see lots of triangles. The famous Eiffel Tower in Paris is a tower of triangles. A bicycle frame made of triangles can support more than ten times its own **weight**.

Materials

The first bikes were made from wood or iron, but today most bikes are made from steel tubes. Steel has enough flexibility (or ability to bend) to stand up to the knocks and bumps of everyday riding. Aluminium is often used instead of steel because it's lighter. Titanium bikes are even lighter and stronger than aluminium bikes, but titanium is very expensive and harder to shape. Some bikes are made of **carbon fibre**, a type of plastic material that is lighter and stronger than steel.

Welding

The parts of a steel bike are joined together by welding. Steel is welded by heating the parts until they melt where they touch. The liquid metal from the two parts runs together and then sets hard as it cools, forming a strong joint.

Forces on Bikes

Forces **are pushes and pulls. They make objects move or change their speed or direction. Forces make bikes go faster, slow down, turn corners and, if you're unlucky, fall over. Some of the forces that act on bikes are forces of nature. Others are forces made by a bike's rider.**

Forces in balance

When a bike is standing still, there are two forces acting on it. **Gravity** pulls the bike downwards. It gives the bike weight. The ground pushes back against the weight of the bike with an upward force. These two forces are perfectly in balance. If they weren't, the bike would fly up into the air or sink into the ground!

Newton's Laws of Motion

Bicycles obey three laws of **motion** discovered by the English scientist, Sir Isaac Newton (1642-1727).

- An object stays still or goes in a straight line at a steady speed unless a force acts on it.
- When a force acts on an object, the object **accelerates** in the direction of the force.
- To every action (force) there is an equal and opposite reaction (another force).

▶ *A bike standing still illustrates both the first and third of Newton's laws of motion. There is no force pushing the bike forwards, so it doesn't accelerate (first law). The bike's weight is balanced by the equal and opposite reaction force from the ground (third law).*

Air resistance

When you ride a bike, two more forces come into play. The first force is made by your feet pushing the pedals round to make the bike move forward. The second force is made by the air around you. When an object moves through air, it has to push the air out of the way. The air pushes back. The pushing force of the air is called **air resistance**, or **drag**. If the pedalling force is bigger than the drag, the bike goes faster. If drag is bigger, the bike slows down. You have to push the pedals harder to cycle into a strong wind, because there is more air resistance to overcome.

▲ *A bike speeds up as it goes downhill, because the force of gravity pulling it down the slope makes it accelerate (Newton's second law of motion).*

Gravity

When you ride a bike on level ground, gravity doesn't affect your speed. When you cycle downhill, however, gravity pulls you down the hill, making you go faster. When you cycle uphill, gravity acts like a brake, slowing you down. That's why it's hard work to cycle uphill and easier to cycle downhill.

Friction

Machines, engines and vehicles of all kinds are affected by a force called friction. Friction tries to stop things from sliding against each other. Some parts of a bike work because of friction. Others work better without it.

What is friction?

If you could look at a smooth surface through a high-power microscope, it would look like a mountain range of peaks and valleys. When two pieces of metal slide against each other, the high peaks in the surfaces hit each other and make it harder for the surfaces to slide. This resistance to sliding is friction. Rougher surfaces catch against each other even more, causing more friction. Friction between the moving parts of a bike acts like a brake, slowing the bike down. It produces a force that acts in the opposite direction to the bike's movement.

▶ *The nuts and bolts that hold a bike together stay tight because of friction.*

Good friction

Some parts of a bike rely on friction. They would not work without it. Friction between the tyres and the ground lets the tyres push against the ground and move a bike. Without friction, the wheels would spin but the bike wouldn't move. Friction makes the brakes work. It also stops your feet from sliding off the pedals and lets you grip the handlebars tightly.

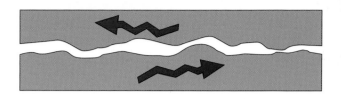

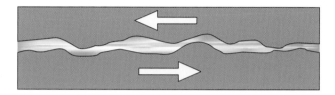

▲ *Friction happens because the rough parts of surfaces hit each other while trying to slide against each other.*

▲ *The addition of oil makes the surfaces slide over each other more easily, and reduces friction.*

▲ *Oil reduces friction between a bike's moving parts so they can move more easily.*

Bad friction

Some parts of a bike have to slide against each other. As the chain goes round, it slides onto teeth by the pedals, then slides off again before sliding on and off the teeth at the back wheel. The pedals and wheels have to turn easily. These moving parts are oiled to make them more slippery. The oil gets between the surfaces so that they don't catch each other as much. Without oil, these parts would rub against each other, slowing the bike down. They would wear away faster too.

Keeping your balance

A bike falls over very easily, so a bike rider has to make small changes in position and steering to stay upright. But what exactly are you doing when you balance on a bike?

Stability

Every object has a point called its **centre of gravity**. The object behaves as if all of its weight is located at that point. The object stays upright if its centre of gravity is above its base. If the object leans over until its centre of gravity moves outside its base, it will fall over.

▲ A bike can be made more stable by adding stabilizers, a small wheel on each side of the back wheel. Stabilizers give a bike a wider base.

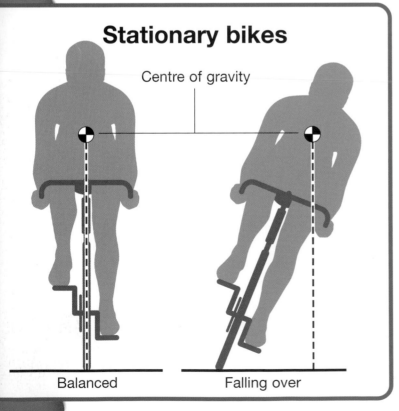

Stationary bikes

Centre of gravity

Balanced

Falling over

For this reason, an object with a wide base and a low centre of gravity is hard to push over. Objects like this are said to be **stable**. A pyramid is very stable. Objects with a small base and a high centre of gravity fall over more easily. They are said to be **unstable**. A pencil standing on its blunt end is unstable. One tiny push and it falls over.

Top heavy

When you ride a bike, most of your weight is at the top of the bike, so your centre of gravity is high. Your base is very small, just the width of the tyres on the ground. You're a bit like a pencil standing on end, very unstable. You have to keep turning the handlebars a little to stay balanced. If the bike starts to fall to one side, you need to steer in that direction to keep your centre of gravity above your base. Maintaining your speed makes it easier to balance.

Gyro-bike

If a bike is given a push and sets off without a rider, it doesn't fall over straight away. How can such an unstable object balance by itself? Its wheels behave like **gyroscopes**.

A gyroscope is a spinning wheel that tries to keep going in the same direction, like a spinning top. When a bike with no rider starts to lean to one side, its front wheel automatically turns in the same direction and stops the bike from falling over. When the bike slows down, the gyroscope and self-steering effects get weaker and weaker until they can't stop the bike from falling over, just like a spinning top falling over when it slows down.

Steering

There's more to steering a bike than just turning the handlebars. Steering involves a tricky balancing act that seems to defy gravity. When you steer a bike around a turn, you are balancing forces that keep changing size and direction.

Make a turn

Imagine you are riding your bike in a straight line and you want to turn right. What do you do? Did you say, 'Turn the handlebars to the right?' If you do that, you'll fall over! When an object moves, it tries to keep going in the same direction. So, if you're riding and you turn the handlebars to the right, the bike turns right but your body tries to keep going straight ahead. As a result, the bike topples over to its left.

Leaning to balance

Leaning into a turn keeps a bike balanced. But how do you make a bike lean over? The easiest way is to shift your weight to one side and let gravity pull the bike over. Another way is to turn the handlebars the wrong way! It may sound strange, but you can make a bike lean over to the right by turning the handlebars to the left! The bike is thrown off balance and it starts to topple. Then, before it falls, turning the handlebars back to the right makes it turn smoothly.

◀ *A rider cannot turn without falling over while a bike is upright. An upright bike can only go straight.*

▲ *It's all in the lean! To make a bike turn, the rider has to make it lean into the turn at exactly the right angle.*

Sliding out

The amount you have to lean a bike over in a turn depends on how fast you're going and how tight the turn is. The faster you go and the tighter the turn, the further you have to lean. But watch out – if you lean over too far, the tyres may lose grip and the bike may slide out from under you!

▼ *Friction stops a bike from falling during a turn, unless the rider leans over too far or the ground is slippery.*

Side-slip

When a bike leans over in a turn, friction between the tyres and the ground stops the bike from sliding sideways. There is less friction when the ground is slippery. That's why it's not safe to lean over as far when you're turning on slippery ground.

Pedal power

Bikes rely on pedals and a chain to get going. The pedals change the pushing force of your leg muscles into a turning force. The chain uses the turning force to move a bike's back wheel.

Torque talk

A turning force is also called **torque**. Pushing a bike's pedals makes a turning force, or torque. Each pedal is at the end of a metal arm called a crank or crank arm. The size of the torque is the force pushing the pedal multiplied by the length of the crank. Long cranks produce more torque than short cranks which makes it easier to push the pedals around.

Chain drive

There are all sorts of different chains. Some are for lifting things, like a ship's anchor. Others are for linking things. A bicycle chain is another type of chain called a drive chain. Leonardo da Vinci first sketched a drive chain in about 1500, but it was another 400 years or so before one was used on a bicycle. A bicycle's pedals turn a wheel called the chain wheel.

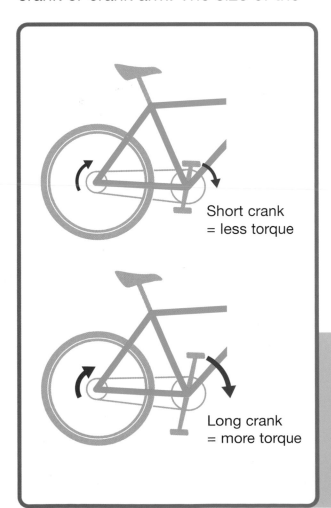

Short crank = less torque

Long crank = more torque

◄ *If these two bikes have the same force applied to their pedals, the bikes with longer cranks will produce more torque. However, cranks can't be too long or the pedals would hit the ground.*

▲ *Driving a bike's back wheel by a chain means that the pedals don't have to be fixed to the middle of the wheel and the rider doesn't have to sit on top of a big front wheel. Positioning the seat lower down between the wheels makes a modern bike easier to ride.*

Teeth around the edge of the chain wheel stick into holes in the chain. Pushing the pedals turns the chain wheel, which pulls the chain around it. The chain then turns another toothed wheel in the middle of the back wheel and this turns the wheel.

Sit up!

It's important that a bike rider sits in the correct position to push the pedals with the biggest force. If your bike seat is too low, you can't push as hard or keep going for as long. Raising the seat makes it easier to pedal harder. If the seat is too high, however, you may not be able to reach the ground when the bike stops.

Ch nging ge .

A bike is easy to ride on level ground, but it gets harder to pedal when you go up a hill. Gears make it easier to keep pedalling at a comfortable speed and with a comfortable force no matter how steep the hill you're climbing.

Force and speed

When you ride a bike up a steep hill, you have to use a lot of force to move the pedals. Riders often stand up on the pedals and use their weight to help push the pedals round. Gears let you change how hard you have to push the pedals around. But there's a price to pay for making it easier to pedal. If you want the bike to keep going at the same speed as before, you'll have to pedal faster. It's your choice – you can push the pedals hard and slow, or change gear and pedal faster with less force.

Gears

A toothed wheel is also called a gearwheel. If two gearwheels the same size are connected by a bicycle chain, they turn at the same speed. If the gears are different sizes, they turn at different speeds. Bike gears let the rider choose a bigger or smaller gearwheel to turn the back wheel. A smaller gearwheel

▲ *Without gears, riding uphill can be a struggle. Standing up adds body weight to the pedalling force.*

at the back makes the back wheel turn faster. A bigger gearwheel makes the back wheel turn more slowly and you do not have to push as hard.

▲ *A set of different-sized gearwheels with an increasing number of teeth, turns the back wheel at different speeds. Changing gear moves the chain from one gearwheel to another.*

Changing gear

How do you change gear? A bike needs a way to move the chain from one gearwheel to another. The most popular bike gears are called derailleur gears. Derailleur means derailing. There is a set of gearwheels, all different sizes, in the middle of the back wheel. To change gear, the rider moves a lever. This makes the chain move sideways so it runs off one gearwheel onto a smaller or bigger gearwheel next to it.

Gear ratio

Count the number of teeth on the chain wheel. Now count the number of teeth on the gearwheel in the middle of the back wheel. Divide the big number by the small number. The answer is a number called the gear ratio. It shows how much the gears speed up the back wheel. If the gear ratio is 2, one turn of the pedals makes the back wheel turn twice.

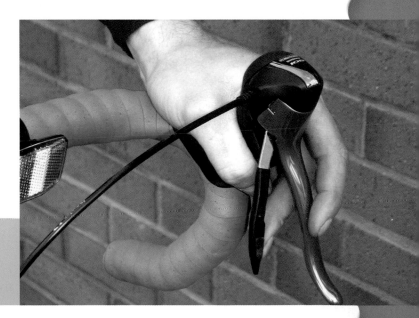

▶ *A bike rider changes gear by moving a lever. The lever pulls a cable, which changes the gear.*

Slow down!

When you want to slow down a fast-moving bike, you need a big force acting backwards. Friction always works in the opposite direction to movement, so it's a good force to use to stop a bike. A bike's brakes work by making a lot of friction.

Slow, slow, stop.

Most bikes have **caliper** brakes. A pad of tough material, such as hard rubber, is held on each side of a wheel. When you are riding, the brake pads do not touch the wheels. When you pull a brake lever, the pads squeeze together and grip the wheel. There is a lot of friction between the brake pads and the wheel. This slows down the wheel.

Slip and slide

Brakes that grip the rims of the wheels don't work well in the rain or when a bike goes through puddles. If water gets between the brake pads and wheels, there is less friction between them, so the bike takes longer to stop. Bikes designed to go through mud and water sometimes have a different type of brake, a disc brake. There is a disc at the centre of each wheel. When you pull the brake lever, a pair of tough pads squeeze together and grip the disc. This slows down the disc and the whole bike.

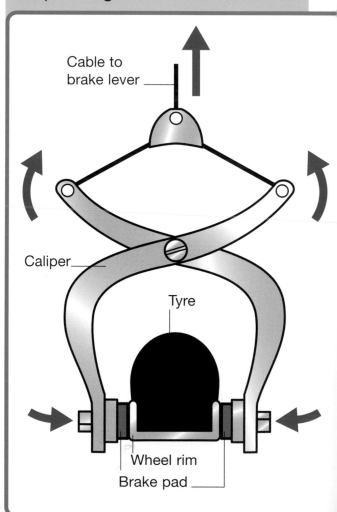

▼ *Pulling the brake lever tugs a cable, which pulls the brake pads on the ends of the calipers together.*

Cable to brake lever

Caliper

Tyre

Wheel rim

Brake pad

The disc doesn't get as wet as the wheel rims when the bike goes through water, because the disc is in the middle of the wheel, so disc brakes work better on wet ground. Another type of bike brake is called the coaster brake. It is located inside the back wheel **hub**. It works when the rider pedals backwards.

Skidding

If you brake too hard, the wheels might suddenly stop turning while the bike is still moving. It makes the wheels skid. When the wheels skid, you can't steer or brake. The bike is out of control and it is very hard to balance.

Energy

You have to produce big forces to push a bike's pedals around, and you need energy to produce these forces. Energy and forces go together. There are different types of energy. When you ride a bike, energy changes from one type to another.

Energy from the Sun

Where does energy come from? It all starts with the Sun. Sunlight gives plants energy to grow. We eat the plants. We also eat meat from animals that eat plants. We take in their energy and store it in our body.

Then our muscles use this energy to produce the forces needed to do all sorts of things, including riding a bike. When something moves, it has a type of energy called **kinetic energy**. A moving bike has kinetic energy. The faster it goes, the more kinetic energy it has.

Potential energy

Riding uphill changes a bike's kinetic energy into a different kind of energy – **potential energy**. An object has potential energy because of where it is. At the top of a hill, for example, a bike has a lot of potential energy. If you let go of the bike's brakes at the top of a hill, the bike starts going down the hill by itself. It is able to start moving because it has potential

◄ *The energy you use to ride a bike comes from food. To keep fit and stay healthy you should eat a well-balanced diet.*

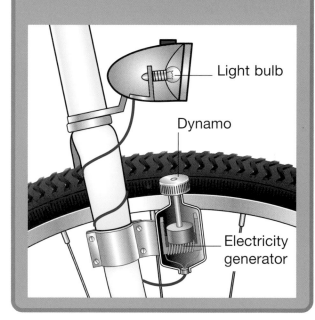

◄ *When you ride a bike, your muscles change chemical energy from your food into kinetic energy.*

Dynamos

A **dynamo** is a small electricity **generator** powered by a bike. A little wheel on the dynamo is pressed against one of the bike's wheels. When the bike moves, the bike wheel turns the dynamo wheel. This drives a small generator that powers the bike's lights. The dynamo changes kinetic energy into electrical energy and then into light energy.

Light bulb

Dynamo

Electricity generator

energy. As the bike runs downhill, its potential energy changes into kinetic energy.

Vanishing energy

Energy can't be created or destroyed. It can only change from one type of energy to another. Scientists call this the 'law of conservation of energy'. If energy can't be destroyed, where does it go when a bike stops? When you stop a bike by using its brakes, friction between the brakes and wheels heats them up. The kinetic energy changes to heat, which is carried away by the surrounding air. There might be a bit of sound energy too, if the brakes squeal.

Wheels and spokes

The centre of a bicycle wheel, the hub, is joined to the rim by pieces of wire called spokes. Bicycle wheels have spokes because spoked wheels are much lighter than solid metal wheels. Reducing weight is important because less force is needed to make light wheels turn.

Forces on wheels

When you sit on a bike, the force of your weight acting downward tries to flatten the wheels. The spokes stop the wheels from collapsing. They help the wheels to keep their circular shape. Half of the spokes go from the rim to one side of the hub. The other half of the spokes go from the rim to the other side of the hub. This gives the wheels extra strength and helps to stop them from folding or buckling. When you start moving, the spokes make the wheels strong enough to withstand pedalling forces and braking forces too.

Push-pull

Bicycle spokes are usually made of thin steel wire. One spoke on its own bends easily, but the same spoke is very hard to stretch or break by pulling at its ends. It is this pulling strength, called **tensile strength**, that makes a spoked wheel so strong. The spokes are tightened so that they pull the rim and hub towards each other with great force. The tightness of the spokes makes a bicycle wheel very stiff and strong.

◄ A bicycle wheel with spokes is amazingly strong. It can support at least 400 times its own weight.

Aero wheels

Bikes for racing on tracks have unusual wheels. Their wheels may be solid or they may have three or four wide, flat spokes. Normal wire spokes stir up the air as a wheel turns, causing a lot of drag (see pages 28-29). A solid wheel, or a wheel with fewer spokes, cuts through the air more cleanly, so it suffers less drag. To save weight, wheels on racing bikes tend to be made from a light material such as carbon fibre.

▼ *Some racing bikes have solid wheels or wheels with wide spokes, because they create less drag. This lets racing cyclists go faster.*

▲ *BMX bikes have small, strong wheels with short spokes to withstand stunts and jumps without bending or breaking.*

Rubber and air

Bikes have had rubber tyres filled with air since John Boyd Dunlop invented the air-filled bicycle tyre in 1888. A bike's tyres support the weight of the bike and rider. They also carry the pedalling and braking forces to the ground.

Rolling resistance

When you sit on a bike, your weight squashes the tyres at the bottom where they rest on the ground. The softer a tyre is, the more your weight squashes it. You have to use more force to turn a wheel with a soft, squashy tyre than a wheel with a hard tyre. The force that slows down a turning wheel is called **rolling resistance**. Hard tyres have less rolling resistance than soft tyres. Racing bikes have thin tyres pumped up to a high **pressure**. The high pressure makes the tyres hard. They squash very little at the bottom, so the wheels have less rolling resistance and the cyclist can go faster.

Fat tyres

Thin hard tyres are no good on soft ground. They sink into soft ground instead of rolling along on top of it. Mountain bikes have fatter, softer tyres. Fat, squashy tyres don't sink into the ground as deeply as thin hard tyres, but they have more rolling resistance. It takes more pedalling force to turn the wheels, so you won't see mountain bikes taking part in a road race like the **Tour de France**!

▶ A road bike's tyres are pumped up to a high pressure, because a bike with hard, high-pressure tyres is easier to pedal than a bike with soft tyres.

24

Tread carefully

The part of a bicycle tyre that touches the ground is called the tread. If you look at a bicycle tyre, you'll see that the tread isn't smooth. A smooth tyre would put the most rubber on the ground, creating the most grip, or friction. But smooth tyres can't grip the ground when it's wet. So, the tread has grooves cut in it. The grooves are called the tread pattern. They let water squeeze out from under a tyre, so that the rest of the tread stays in contact with the ground.

▲ *Tyres with a knobbly tread grip soft, uneven ground well because the big bumps in the tread dig into the ground.*

▶ *The grooves in a bicycle tyre are there to squeeze water out from under the tyre and stop it from aquaplaning, or hydroplaning.*

Aquaplaning

On wet ground, water can get between the ground and a smooth tyre. The tyre actually ends up floating on top of a thin film of water. If the tyre doesn't touch the ground, there is no friction between them and the tyre loses grip. This is called aquaplaning or hydroplaning (bottom).

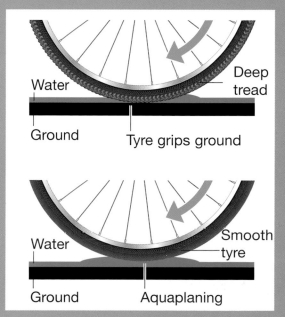

Water

Ground

Deep tread

Tyre grips ground

Water

Ground

Smooth tyre

Aquaplaning

Smoothing out bumps

Some early bikes were called boneshakers because of the way their wooden wheels with iron tyres rattled over bumps. All the shaking made the bikes hard to ride. Thank goodness modern bikes are more comfortable to ride than old-fashioned boneshakers!

Springy air

Modern bikes 'soak up' or absorb bumps better than old boneshakers because they have rubber tyres full of air. Rubber is flexible and air can be squashed like a spring. When a bike's wheel rolls over a small bump, the bump squashes the tyre. The air inside the tyre is squashed too, and then it springs back.

Springs and things

A bike's tyres soak up small bumps, but bikes made for riding on rough ground and bikes made for doing stunts often have extra ways of soaking up bigger bumps. They have springs that let the wheels bounce up farther when they go over big bumps. A big spring, however, would keep bouncing up and down after a bike had gone over a bump. To stop this, the spring is coiled around another part called a **damper** or **shock absorber**. This lets the spring squash fast, but slows it down as it bounces back.

Suspension

A bike's springs and dampers are also called its **suspension** system. A bike might have no suspension, front suspension only, or front-and-back

▼ *A bike with front suspension only is known as a hardtail.*

suspension. Front suspension is usually inside the front **fork**, the part that holds the front wheel in position. It lets the front wheel move up and down. Rear suspension is usually provided by a big spring and shock absorber under the seat.

> ▶ *A bike with suspension at the front and back is said to be a* **full-suspension bike**.

Rear suspension

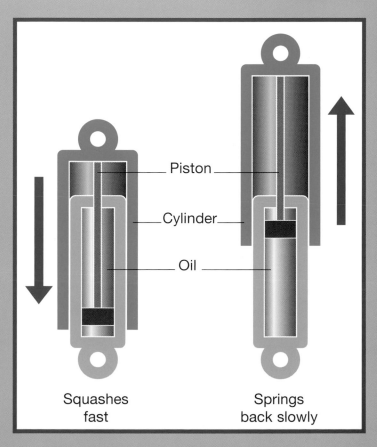

Piston

Cylinder

Oil

Squashes
fast

Springs
back slowly

Inside a shock absorber

A shock absorber is a tube full of air or oil, with a piston inside it, a bit like a bicycle pump. Hold your finger over the end of a bicycle pump and push the handle to feel the springiness of the air inside. When a bike goes over a bump, the shock absorber is squashed fast, but the air or oil inside it makes it spring back more slowly.

Pushing air

The scientific study of objects moving through air is called aerodynamics. Aerodynamics is an important part of designing the shape of fast vehicles like aeroplanes. It is also important in the design of fast bikes. Changing a bike's shape can let it speed through the air faster.

What a drag!

When you ride a bike, you push yourself and the bike through the air. The air pushes back, creating air resistance, or drag. Two types of drag affect bike riders. One is caused by pushing against the air in front of you. This is called pressure drag. As the air flows around you, it rubs against you. This causes the second type of drag, called skin friction. Pressure drag slows you down a lot more than skin friction does.

Racing faster

Racing cyclists try to go as fast as possible, not only by having the best bikes and pedalling fast, but also by reducing drag. Their bikes are made from oval or teardrop-shaped tubes instead of round tubes. Oval and teardrop-shaped tubes let air flow around them more easily. Some racing bikes have a plastic body, because a smooth plastic body causes less drag than a frame made of tubes. Wheels with spokes stir up the air and cause a lot of drag, so some racing bikes have solid wheels.

◀ *Low handlebars make a rider bend over lower into a position that lets air flow over his head and back more smoothly, reducing drag. Shapes that let air flow around them smoothly are called* **streamlined** *shapes.*

Slipstreaming

Racing cyclists can keep going fast without having to pedal as hard by doing something called slipstreaming. A cyclist pushing against the air, raises the air pressure in front of him and lowers the air pressure behind him. Another cyclist will try to get close enough to the rider in front, so he can ride inside this pocket of low-pressure air. Now, the second cyclist has low pressure air in front of him. This reduces his pressure drag and so he doesn't have to pedal as hard. Slipstreaming lets the leading rider do the work of overcoming drag, while the following rider saves energy for later in the race. If you watch a team of racing cyclists, you'll see each of them take the lead for a while to do the hard work while the others tuck in close behind.

▲ *Racing cyclists often wear a skintight suit to reduce skin friction so that they can go faster. A streamlined helmet helps too.*

▼ *Racing cyclists ride close together because it cuts drag and saves energy.*

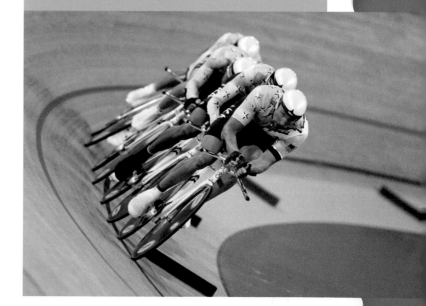

Glossary

accelerate go faster

air resistance a force that slows something down as it moves through air, caused by the air pushing back against the moving object

caliper a device with two arms that can be squeezed together, like a pair of scissors; used in bike brakes

carbon fibre a very light, but strong material made from hair-thin strands of carbon embedded in plastic

centre of gravity the point where gravity pulls an object, as if all of the object's weight was concentrated at that one point

damper shock absorber

drag air resistance

dynamo a small electricity generator used by a bicycle to make electricity for its lights

force something that makes an object accelerate or change shape

fork the part of a bike that holds the front wheel in position: it looks like a fork with two prongs, one on each side of the wheel

full-suspension bike a bike with front and rear suspension

generator a machine that changes motion into electric current

gravity a force that pulls everything towards an object with mass, such as the Earth

gyroscope a spinning wheel that tries to keep going in the same way, like a spinning top

hub the centre part of a wheel

kinetic energy a type of energy possessed by a moving object

motion movement

potential energy a type of energy stored in an object that has the potential to be released or converted into other forms of energy

pressure pressing or squeezing

recumbent lying down; a recumbent bike has a lying-down riding position

rolling resistance a force that tries to stop a wheel from moving

shock absorber a device for soaking up sudden jolts and bumps to give a smoother ride

stable likely to stay upright, hard to topple

streamlined having a shape that lets air flow around it smoothly

suspension the springs and shock absorbers that give a smooth ride on bumpy ground

tensile strength the resistance of a material to breaking under tension

torque a force that makes something turn

Tour de France the world's most famous bicycle race

unstable unlikely to stay upright, easy to topple

weight the heaviness of an object, caused by gravity pulling it towards the centre of the Earth

Websites

The Exploratorium's Science of Cycling
www.exploratorium.edu/cycling

This museum website has information about bicycle science.

How Stuff Works: How Bicycles Work
http://science.howstuffworks.com/bicycle.htm

This site explains the basics of how bikes work.

http://travel.howstuffworks.com/mountain-bike.htm

This site explains the science behind mountain bikes.

A Quick History of Bicycles
www.pedalinghistory.com/PHhistory.html

This museum website includes a short history of bicycles.

Note to parents and teachers: *Every effort has been made by the publishers to ensure that these websites are suitable for children, that they are of the highest educational value, and that they contain no inappropriate or offensive material. However, because of the nature of the Internet, it is impossible to guarantee that the contents of these sites will not be altered. We strongly advise that Internet access is supervised by a responsible adult.*

Index